THE SCOTTISH
COUNTRYSIDE

in Pictures

IN GLEN SHIEL, ON THE OLD ROAD TO SKYE

MUCH of the road through Glen Shiel runs in the shadow of those noble mountain peaks known as the Five Sisters of Kintail. At Bridge of Shiel, near the head of Loch Duich, this ancient drove-road continues Skye-wards, via the formidable mountain pass of Mam Ratagan and Glen Elg, to the narrows at Kylerhea.

THE SCOTTISH COUNTRYSIDE

in Pictures

FOREWORD AND INTRODUCTIONS BY F. FRASER DARLING

ILLUSTRATIONS DESCRIBED BY ALASDAIR ALPIN MACGREGOR

CONTENTS

*

W. W. NORTON & COMPANY, INC. · NEW YORK

BORDER COUNTRY

THE Border Country is essentially the land of Sir Walter Scott. One can scarcely move about it without arriving at some spot rendered memorable by him—the Eildons, Sandy Knowe, Smailholm, the Tweed, the Gala Water, the Border abbey towns of Kelso, Jedburgh, Melrose, and Dryburgh. The landscape of the Borders, interwoven so closely with their history, he bequeathed to the world of books as surely and irrevocably as any writer, by his craft, ever bequeathed anything.

4

Foreword

THE art of seeing country is part of the art of being a traveller. Successful travellers are all too rare. Take R. L. Stevenson's *Travels With a Donkey*: he did remarkably little that was out of the ordinary, yet he produced a classic of travel. This and many others of his books show a delight in country for its own sake and are worth reading as lessons in seeing what is before our eyes as we move about. Then comes the more polished accomplishment of deduction and inference from what we see. Such a traveller is becoming a connoisseur, taking his country like choice wine, slowly and appreciatively, with cultivated reflection. Great gulps of fast movement through new country are an offence against good taste.

I am counselling perfection. Coming down to brass tacks, one cannot seriously advise travel in Scotland with a Modestine; asses are excessively rare in that country and we are too late in time. All the same, I have always promised myself a tour on the hill tracks of the Highlands with a pack pony and this is a reasonable idea, for Highland ponies are douce beasts and could be hired outside the limits of the stalking season. Just plain walking, you may say, is the best way of seeing country and I entirely agree, as long as it is plain walking and not humping a rucksack piled high with gear. The hiker looks at the earth and during his necessary rests lies on his back and closes his tired eyes, or gazes into the sky.

The car and the cycle hold the day and most of us are grateful for what they can give. They are good servants and bad masters. Speed and mileage are not their end if we are to know Scotland; they should get us somewhere where we can get out and make the best use of our legs and eyes.

The picture book made by the camera can in some measure interpret the seeing eye of one particular traveller or, as here, the sudden vision of many who saw beauty and wished to capture it. There is still the connecting thread of the editor's choice running through, and perhaps the best way of compiling an illustrated book is to get all the illustrations first and write round them. The extended caption to a chosen photograph can be a revealing and economical form. It tells, and yet leaves plenty of room for the reader's own imagination to play. Such a book can make for good arm-chair travelling, recapturing an experience or inspiring an exploration.

Scotland is a country of immense variety and of many distinctive qualities. The inquiring mind will attempt to analyse these things and then to re-synthesize them into appreciation of people, landscape, architecture, industries and crafts and everyday life and busy-nesses. That shrewd Scotsman and commentator on his own race, Ian Finlay, has called Romanticism "Scotland's Old Man of the Sea," and the romantic attachment so commonly extolled as "the fickle glue." The phrases are happy ones: the beauty of Scotland should not be approached in that way. Let the ultimate romance grow from a soil of reality. This book deals with the Scottish countryside and therefore does not pretend to portray the whole of Scotland. You will see the beauty of the Firth of Clyde, but not Govan or the Broomielaw farther up the river. The shale bings of West Lothian are not shown, nor the pitheads of Cowdenbeath in Fife, yet both of those counties hold some of the loveliest things in Scotland. The book is concerned with the countryside and quieter scene in village and small town, where heritage is easier to see, and the development of Scottish life. Seen aright, our wits should be sharpened and our love rekindled, so that we may the surer take care of the beautiful things we have. This would be humility, not romanticism.

We have the axiom that Scotland is a country of variety and sharp contrasts. First the people: we have three races present at least, and two cultures, and the combinations of these lead to both fusions and impacts. There is the Saxon of the Southern Uplands and Border country, the Norseman of the Shetland and Orkney Islands and of the north-east coast, and the Gael of the Highlands and Western Isles. Saxon and Norseman in Scotland have fused closer than Wessex Saxon and Dane have done in England and identify themselves with each other much more than the Yorkshireman and man of Devon would do. Most non-Highland Scots are unaware of any differences of origin, and would find the fact of little consequence.

Things are different in the Highlands. And yet the Highlander is not a true Gael by blood. The Outer Isles, Skye and the north and north-west coasts were conquered by the Norseman before the Norman Conquest of Britain. Indeed, by that time there had been established in the West the Norse-Celtic kingdom of the Lordship of the Isles, but the Norse of the West accepted the culture of the Gaels they conquered. Place-names in the Highlands and Islands show in many parts a preponderance of Norse origins, yet the Gaelic culture persisted, so that now the man from the West who looks every inch a Norseman will speak Gaelic and think as a Gael, not as a Zetlander or Orcadian, and still less like a Lowland Scotsman. It is the fashion to minimize the differences between Highlander and Lowlander, but the fact remains they are far apart in habit of mind. The Highlander is subtle, sensitive, intuitive and difficult to pin down to definite statements. The Lowlander likes to be definite, practical and full of common sense. The two cultures tend to despise each other, though a minority of each idealizes the ways of the other, and most Lowlanders who have it like to boast of Highland blood.

6

THE SALISBURY CRAGS, EDINBURGH

SCOTLAND'S capital possesses in the King's Park a public pleasance of unusual grandeur. At its centre, and rising to a height of 822 feet, stands that well-known landmark, Arthur's Seat. Along the western side of the highlands comprising the greater part of the Park are the Salisbury Crags, from the top of which one obtains an intimate view of Old Edinburgh.

The Lowlander is the great farmer and reclaimer of land and the pastoralist in a big way. The true crofter has practically disappeared from non-Highland Scotland, but in the West Highlands and Hebrides the crofter or peasant holder persists. He has his two or three acres of inbye land and shares a common grazing on the hill. In more than half the crofting townships the land is laid open to the township stock in winter, which means that no true farming can develop. The Highlander prefers it so, but the Lowlander thinks such a primitive survival quite daft. Who knows? The traveller in the Highlands will also see traces of earlier inhabitants in the present population, especially examples of the dark Iberian type, whose ancestors may have built the great stone circle of Callernish on the west side of Lewis.

The art of seeing country is greatly helped by even an elementary appreciation of the main geological characters and events. Different kinds of rock make different qualities of scenery and types of growth, and the fact that Scotland suffered four periods of glaciation has had a profound influence on scenery and on the uses to which we put the land today. In the far north-west and in the Outer Hebrides much of the landscape is composed of the oldest rock in the world, the Archaean gneiss; it is extremely hard and has been much scoured by the ice, so that now we have nobbly little hills where the rock shows bare in seemingly more than half the area in view. Soil is almost non-existent. Obviously, this is no place for high farming, and as the rock bears no valuable minerals we cannot expect to see any signs of big industry. It is, in fact, the most sparsely inhabited area in Scotland.

INVERNESS, FROM THE CASTLE

THE little town of Inverness, situated on both banks of the River Ness where it enters the Beauly Firth, is placed by the shore of one of the loveliest estuaries in the world. The surrounding countryside is for the most part rich, arable land, producing some of the finest grain crops in Britain. Being but a few miles from Culloden, where the Jacobites were defeated in 1746, it treasures its associations with Prince Charlie.

At the other extreme there is the red sandstone of Dunbar and Cockburnspath, a rock which drains easily, breaks down into beautiful rich soil and has easy slopes. There is no better farming in Scotland than here, where the famous red-soil potatoes are grown.

A gigantic earth movement of cracking and slipping produced one of the major features of Scottish geography, the Great Glen, stretching from Inverness south-westwards to Loch Linnhe. This magnificent glen, absolutely straight and ninety miles long, holding in Loch Ness the largest mass of fresh water in Scotland, is of quite different character from the numerous U-shaped glens which are formed by the gouging action of glaciers. There is also the Highland Border Fault, almost but not quite parallel with the Great Glen, stretching from Stonehaven to the mouth of the Clyde. This is the "Highland Line" of history.

The west coast of Scotland is like a jig-saw puzzle in its intricate maze of islands and long sea-lochs. Each year these narrow waters are sailed by numerous small yachts, and that is the best way to see the character and structure of this part of Scotland. The roads are long, narrow and poor and do not get the traveller to vantage points as easily as the yachts and steamers. The observant eye will see along this west coast the striking influence of the long-gone ice. Several thousand feet thickness of ice is quite a depressing thing—at least it kept the land "hauden doon." Then, when it melted, it raised the level of the sea and "drowned" the coastline, making it possible for us now to take quite big ships close inshore among the lochs and sounds. But the freedom from weight of ice then allowed the land to rise a little, and this accounts for the numerous "raised beaches" at twenty-five, fifty and a hundred feet, which are now often enough the arable strips of crofting townships.

Volcanoes have also played their part in forming the scenery of Scotland: Arthur's Seat is perhaps the best known, as it is the most prominent landmark in the neighbourhood of Edinburgh, and a fine isolated hill. On the other side of the country there is magnificent volcanic scenery in Mull, Morven and Skye, the most perfect small example being the Dutchman's Cap, the southernmost of the Treshnish Isles and only 284 feet high. These volcanoes were active about fifty million years ago. Scotland, indeed, has been the site of great geological turmoil and she was being squeezed and gouged under the ice when Palaeolithic man was colonizing a South of England that never knew such a scourge. All this we interpret today in grandeur of scenery, but it has been paid for over more than half the country in loss of soil, and when man came finally to Scotland it was to a country that the healing powers of nature had been able to make good only in part.

The climate of Scotland has much to do with scenery and with life and work as well. The west side is very wet and the east of Scotland is dry; the west is much milder than the east in winter and the summers are, in general, cooler; the west is subject to too many heavy gales from the south-west, but the dry, crisp east coast can take no great liberties because the easterly gales of winter and spring can be shriving experiences. This variation of conditions allows within the bounds of Scotland the sub-tropical garden at Logan on the Mull of Galloway and the arctic-alpine complex of vegetation on the Cairngorm plateaux.

Climate does much to make scenery beautiful or otherwise, and in this respect Scotland usually gains. The quality of light and the state of humidity of the atmosphere give an ecstatic quality to the Highlands and Southern Uplands. The calm, cold weather after snow gives something to Scotland which England seems not to get. Again it is ecstatic.

Climate has also affected Scottish architecture by pruning it and keeping it more severe, both in the domestic and ecclesiastical fields. Some of the great houses of Scotland and such small towns as St. Andrews and Culross show how an almost functional plainness can still achieve beauty. Churches rarely go beyond the virtuosity of the hollow spire—which is a beautiful and homely thing to a Scotsman.

And with architecture let us link the quiet, intimate gardens of many of the older houses. Perhaps the sterner landscape beyond drew forth this quiet art of the Scottish gardener and gave these pleasances their distinction.

F. Fraser Darling.

THE BUTT OF LEWIS

NOT unlike the rocky and precipitous coast of Caithness is that of Ness, the northernmost parish of Lewis, in the Outer Hebrides, which terminates in that lofty promontory known as the Butt of Lewis, upon which stands the lighthouse of the same name. Ness is a typical Hebridean crofting region, and, for all its poverty in natural resources, it carries a considerable population, whose livelihood is supplemented by fishing. The rounded arch tunnelled by the sea through the rock at the very tip of the Butt is called the "eye" of the Butt. Through this "eye," tradition says, the Norse ran their ropes when endeavouring to tow the Island of Lewis over the North Sea to Norway.

The Highlands
and Islands

THE Highlands and Western Isles of Scotland are the largest expanse of rough country in Britain—and they are the roughest country. It is possible to go from the foot of the Great Glen or Ardnamurchan to the north coast without a fence to stop you; one hundred and fifty miles as the crow flies.

There are 543 summits over three thousand feet in height in the Highlands, the most southerly ones being Ben Lomond, Ben Vorlich and Stuc a'Chroin, all within thirty-fifty miles of Edinburgh and Glasgow. The Cobbler, not quite three thousand feet, gives as good climbing as you could wish, and is no farther away. On these hills young Scotland learns how to get about and look after itself, then with a thrill it goes farther north into the great Glen Coe complex of very dangerous hills. And there is enough historical romance round there to last a lifetime. Then, when young Scotland is slightly older and with a few shillings more in the pocket, the journey is made to the Coolins of Skye, those incomparable hills of gabbro which are for the connoisseur in climbing. In the great granite mass of plateaux of the Cairngorm hills you can walk and be unashamed of being a walker, however hard your climbing may be tested, if you wish, but in the Coolins you can't walk far anyway; you just climb.

If you want to see this aspect of the Highlands in the sense of vastness, climb a high hill like Ben Alder or Craig Meagaidh, or possibly a smaller one farther west, say Ben Resipol, where you can see well out to sea and to the Hebrides. You will see the summits going on and on and on, all round you from the first two, and on three sides from the third, the west side here being made up of that wonderful coastline which surely only the classical coasts of Greece can equal.

But this vastness and on-and-on quality of the Highlands is only one aspect of the country. There is the remoteness you can feel at the head of some glen sitting by a rowan tree where the river starts as a trickle. And there is the nostalgic quality of the western sea, and the life of the people of the islands. The whole western edge of the Highlands is intimately bound up with the sea because of the tortuous coastline. The people live at the sea's edge for the most part, even if their living is not gained from the sea: even on the large pastoral island of Skye there is only one township as far as three miles from the sea, and the rest of the islanders poke fun at the folk of Glenmore. It was a Glenmore man, they tell you, who when out in a roughish sea asked the man at the tiller to keep the boat along the hollows!

There is also the matter of the ocean—something quite different from mere sea-water. If you know the shores of the Minch and of Skye you will know how different the sea is from that which rolls on the beaches of Tiree and of the Uists and pounds the cliffs of Gallan Head. The majesty of the Atlantic Ocean experienced from these farthest shores is immense and wonderful, whereas the short chop from the Minch is either just pretty, or, if you are afloat, annoying. The Atlantic has the full, deep rhythm; the rollers are long and cream far up the white beaches of the Isles or crash in a column of spray against skerry and cliff.

These outer beaches of the Hebrides need special mention. They are composed of shell-sand, not pulverized rock, which accounts for their cream colour. Millions of tons over many thousands of years have been thrown up and blown up, until a belt of a few hundred yards to two miles wide is formed, or, in the case of the low island of Tiree, the shell-sand has blown right across the island. Shell-sand is rich in lime, which is good for the growth of grass and many other plants, so that on the west side of the Hebrides we find a wide stretch of grassland on the sand which flattens out into a level or undulating plain behind the rampart of the dunes which flank the actual beaches. The *machair* is the jewel of the islands, studded with innumerable flowers in July, and green the year through. The greater number of the people live on or near the *machair*, for the rich limy pasture means life for their animals. Also, it is pleasant there; your feet walk dry because the sandy soil drains so well, there is the light, and the ocean. How different from the louring cloudiness of the mainland glens that depend on other tricks of light for their beauty!

We have dwelt rather on space and bareness in looking from the hill summits and along the island shores. But there is a leafy, bosky aspect of the Highlands as well. Give shelter from the great tempests and see what another world arises; if you turn into Loch Sunart from the wild point of Ardnamurchan you will see the shores clothed with woods of oak and birch. On the exposed Atlantic island of Colonsay a seaward cliff protects a little glen running north and south where, round an old Georgian house, are gardens and wooded policies that transport one to Southern England in a moment.

That, I think, is what strikes the reason most forcibly in thinking of the Highlands, the quality of contrast and paradox. The golden eagle flies in a higher reach of the same air as the speckled wood butterfly. In the great Inverness-shire glens of Affric and Cannich, where there is old pine forest and the big rivers run fast, you might be in parts of Canada. Not so far west in the Inverewe garden it might be Teneriffe, but on the *machairs* you can be nowhere else but where you are.

FISHING BOATS AT BRODICK, ISLE OF ARRAN

BUTESHIRE is a county consisting wholly of islands. It embraces Bute, Arran, and the Cumbraes, together with the lesser isles of Holy Island, Pladda, and Inchmarnock. Arran is the most beautiful and diversified of them. It possesses mountains and cliffs well worthy of the most intrepid mountaineer and rock-climber and, indeed, neglected by neither. Brodick, situated on the fringe of the bay of that name, and overlooked by Goat Fell (2,866 feet), is Arran's chief centre of population and activity. Fishing is prosecuted in the neighbouring sea-ways by local crews owning the smaller type of herring-drifter seen above.

ARRAN, SEEN FROM DAVAAR

ONE of the most extensive views of Arran is
that to be had from the east side of Kintyre.
Its hills, seen from as far south as Davaar
Island, are remarkably impressive across
the Kilbrennan Sound. The lofty Davaar,
situated at the entrance to Campbeltown
Loch, is roughly a mile and a half in circum-
ference. It is connected with the mainland
of Kintyre by a long, low ridge of sand and
shingle known as the Dorlin, along which
one may pass dryshod at low tide. Some sheep
graze upon its heathery pastures, but it has
no human inhabitants except those associated with the lighthouse, built at its northern end in 1854 in order to prevent mari-
ners unfamiliar with these sea-ways from
attempting to make the port of Campbeltown by the south end when the Dorlin was
covered by the tide.

THE KYLES OF BUTE

IF THERE be one thing of which the citizens of Glasgow are justly proud, it is the facility with which they can sail down the Clyde—"doon the watter," as the saying is—in their own Clyde-built steamers. Few cities are as favourably situated as is Glasgow for a day's cruise almost from one's own doorstep into the heart of the loveliest scenery imaginable. One has but to travel to Inveraray from the centre of this vast and everexpanding metropolis to realize how unsurpassed is the beauty of the Firth of Clyde and particularly, perhaps, the beauty of the Kyles of Bute, those narrows separating the island of Bute from that part of the mainland of Argyllshire known as Cowal, the ancient patrimony of the Clan Lamont. Once Ardlamont Point, the south-western extremity of Cowal, has been rounded, the vessel enters Loch Fyne, at its mouth, to sail northwards up that romantic sea-loch to Inveraray, county town of Argyllshire. At the time of the celebrated Glasgow Fair holidays, tens of thousands sail to Inveraray by way of the Kyles of Bute.

15

GLEN ROSA AND THE PEAK OF CIR MHOR

ARRAN, possessing as it does so many fine mountains, has an equal number of fine glens. Nowhere in Scotland, except perhaps in the Cairngorms, is there such splendid rock-climbing as in Arran, a fact fully appreciated by the Scottish Mountaineering Club, whose admirable guide-book sets forth all that the lover of the wide, open spaces might wish to learn about its mountains and rock-faces, its glens and tumbling cataracts.

APPROACHING THE PIER AT DUNOON, ARGYLL

MUCH of the Cowal peninsula, which lies between the Firth of Clyde and Loch Fyne, is as inaccessible as any part of the Western Highlands. In contrast with its remoter parts is Dunoon, the largest and busiest centre of Argyll, which to the Clydesider is what Brighton is to the Londoner. The locality is rich in historical associations, though the merest ruins remain of the castle where the Constables of Dunoon lived in so regal a style.

OBAN, THE WEST HIGHLAND CAPITAL

"KING GEORGE V" AT OBAN

OBAN is the most fashionable watering-place in the Highlands. Its fine, sheltered bay, and the numerous beautiful sea-ways within easy reach, have made it a yachting centre of considerable importance. The hills behind the town command one of the finest panoramas of the coast and islands in Britain. One of a fine fleet of fast and luxurious pleasure steamers sailing from Oban is *King George V*, seen above, which circumnavigates the island of Mull, passes close to Fingal's Cave, Staffa, and enables passengers to spend an hour or two ashore at Iona, before returning to Oban in the late afternoon.

LOCH AWE AND THE CLYDE

IN THE heart of Argyllshire lies Loch Awe, the north-east end of which is dominated by the imposing mass of Ben Cruachan (3,689 feet), and there, on a spit of land in the shadow of the great Ben, and still somewhat inaccessible, especially in time of winter flood, stand the ruins of Kilchurn Castle (*right*). The five-storeyed keep, the ruins of which we see today, stand on a site once occupied by a fortress of the Clan Gregor. It was built by Sir Colin Campbell, a Knight of Rhodes, and founder of the historic family of Breadalbane, in 1440, though Highland tradition says it was erected by Sir Colin's lady while her husband was absent in Palestine on a Crusade. In contrast with the solitude of Loch Awe is the Firth of Clyde during the "Clyde Fortnight" (*below*), when many of the most beautiful yachts in the world may be seen in contest upon one of the world's most beautiful sea-ways.

PRINCE CHARLIE'S MONUMENT AT GLENFINNAN, LOCH SHIEL

THE PIER AT HUNTER'S QUAY

FOUR names well known to Glasgow citizens who holiday in Cowal are Innellan, Dunoon, Kirn, and Hunter's Quay. The last mentioned, which, together with Kirn, forms part of the ever-growing burgh of Dunoon, perpetuates the name of John Hunter of Hafton, who did much to develop this locality as a centre likely to attract Clyde-built steamers bringing holiday-makers from Glasgow. It is a well-known yachting centre.

LOCH ECK, ARGYLL

THE Cowal district of Argyll, although it possesses many fine sea-lochs, has only one inland loch of any size, namely, Loch Eck. This lovely loch lies narrowly between the mountains for a distance of over six miles between Strachur, on Loch Fyne, and the head of the Holy Loch, on the overland route from Glasgow to the Cowal coast via Loch Lomond, Glen Croe, and the tortuous mountain road culminating at "Rest and be Thankful."

ARDNAMURCHAN POINT is the most westerly reach of the Scottish mainland. There stands the lighthouse (*left*) which is so well known to all who sail the seas between the mainland and the Inner Hebrides. Farther south, in Appin, are the ruins of the thirteenth-century Castle Stalker (*below*), used by James IV of Scotland as a hunting seat after it had been restored by his kinsman, Duncan Stewart. The road running southward from Oban, if pursued far enough, will lead by

way of Kilninver, Ardrishaig, and Tarbert to the Mull of Kintyre. At Kilninver the road sends off a branch in a south-westerly direction towards Seil, one of the many islands in the beautiful Firth of Lorne. At Clachan Bridge (*right*), said to be the only bridge over the Atlantic, this branch road is carried across the narrow channel to Seil itself, an island of nearly four thousand acres, once more noted for its slate quarries than it is today. Varieties of clay slate form the larger part of Seil.

THE GRANDEUR OF GLEN COE

THOUGH more than two and a half centuries have gone by since the MacDonalds were traitorously done to death in their homes by their guests, the Campbells, memories of the tragedy are revived when, on each anniversary, a memorial service is held in Gaelic at the monument situated near the foot of the Glen (*left*). The picture above shows the Glen Coe hills from Rannoch Moor, regarded by many as the dreariest locality in Scotland. Open, solitary, and silent, the very birds would appear to shun it. Deer find but little sustenance upon it. All attempts to cultivate it have failed.

28

THE PASS OF GLEN COE

MACAULAY called Glen Coe "the most dreary and melancholy of all Scotland's passes—the very Valley of the Shadow of Death." Nevertheless there can be little doubt that it is one of the finest glens in Scotland. It lies in northern Argyll, between great and majestic mountains, and through it tumbles the River Cona of Ossianic memory. In the flank of Aonach Dubh, one of its massive mountains, is Ossian's Cave, and the old folks still declare that the Fingalians hunted the red deer in the Glen's steep corries. The scene in this part of Argyll is often enhanced by straying herds of Highland cattle, those shaggy, soft-eyed creatures without which the Highland wastelands would be incomplete.

THE GLEN COE HILLS AND LOCH LEVEN

TARBERT, LOCH FYNE

DELIGHTFULLY situated at the head of East Loch Tarbert, an inlet of Loch Fyne, is the prosperous village of Tarbert. It is usually referred to as Tarbert, Loch Fyne, in order to distinguish it from Tarbert, Harris, a village in the Outer Hebrides, very similarly situated. The name, Tarbert (or Tarbet), denotes an isthmus across which the Norsemen of old dragged their boats from one bit of water to another. Here they dragged them across the narrow neck of land linking Knapdale and Kintyre, between East Loch Tarbert and West Loch Tarbert, thus dispensing with the necessity of sailing round the Mull of Kintyre, many miles to the south'ard. Travellers to the island of Islay disembark at Tarbert and travel overland to West Loch Tarbert, whence the Islay steamer plies to Port Ellen and Port Askaig alternately.

32

CAPITAL OF ARGYLL

THOUGH Lochgilphead is the administrative centre of Argyll, and holds the principal County Council offices, Inveraray has long been its capital. This little town is one of the sweetest in the Highlands. At its centre stands the Old Parish Church, with its iron-studded doors. It is, in fact, two churches: a partition about its middle divides it in two, each with a pulpit of its own. Here, on the Sabbath, while a service in English is being conducted at one end of the building, the Gaelic-speaking members of the parish are congregating at the other, for public worship in the ancient tongue of the Gael begins immediately after the conclusion of the diet in English. On the town's outskirts stands Inverary Castle, designed by Robert Adam, seat of the Duke of Argyll. A feature of Inveraray well worth mentioning is the great peal in the Belfry Tower at All Saints', a prosperous unit of the Scottish Episcopal Church.

THE ISLAND OF BARRA

UP UNTIL 1939, Castlebay was one of the principal herring-fishing ports on the west coast of Scotland. However, owing to its remoteness, the fishing industry there has declined, and the fishermen now land their catches at Mallaig or at Oban. In the height of the season the population of Barra was increased by curers, coopers, and gutters who came from the mainland to handle the great catches. Situated on a rocky islet within earshot of the pier at Castlebay are the ruins of Kisimul Castle, once the stronghold of the MacNeils of Barra, those daring Hebridean pirates whose excesses troubled not only King James VI of Scotland, but also Queen Elizabeth. The castle's great strength in olden times lay in its being accessible only by water, an advantage appreciated by its turbulent occupants, who were accounted the most skilful seamen of their day. Like most of the Hebrides, Barra possesses large peat deposits, which provide the islanders with a limitless source of fuel. A spell of fine weather calls them out to the peat bogs, where they continue to cut the peats for the coming winter as long as daylight lasts.

SKYE: MOST ROMANTIC OF SCOTTISH ISLANDS

SKYE possesses in the Coolins one of the finest mountain groups in the world. This is shown by the fact that experienced mountaineers and rock-climbers, anxious to test sureness of foot upon their more dangerous and inaccessible parts, visit them from all over the globe. From Elgol, on the south-eastern shores of that well-known sea-loch, Loch Scavaig (*above*), a very fine view of the Coolins can be obtained. But half a mile to the north of Loch Scavaig is Loch Coruisk (*top, left*), a freshwater loch lying deep among the Coolins. To be fully appreciated, it ought to be seen on a dull, foreboding day, when towering clouds would appear to brush its inky-black surface. Seen under such conditions, no one would dare question the existence of the *uruisg*, or hobgoblin, said to haunt its depths. On a green eminence overlooking the Minch, in Trotternish, the northernmost province of Skye, stand the ruins of Duntulm Castle (*left*) which, for at least two centuries, was the chief seat of the dauntless Lords of the Isles. They were obliged to abandon it, it is said, on account of the haunting ghost of one of their illustrious kinsmen, Donald Gorm MacDonald. The ruins one sees today are the merest fragment of a stronghold once unassailable by land or by sea.

SGURR NAN GILLEAN, SKYE

TOBERMORY, ISLE OF MULL

By the shore of a bay at the north end of Mull is situated Tobermory—"Mary's Well"—the island's principal centre of population and activity. Tobermory Bay is known to seekers of treasure all over the world. There, in 1588, a galleon of the Spanish Armada was sunk with what was believed to be untold wealth. At varying intervals ever since, divers, with but meagre results, have sought to recover treasure from the sunken wreck.

LEWIS CASTLE, STORNOWAY, ISLE OF LEWIS

TODAY not a vestige is to be seen of the Lewis Castle of former centuries. Its site lies concealed beneath the heavy timbers of No. 1 Wharf at Stornoway, where this photograph was taken. The last fragments of it were demolished nearly three-quarters of a century ago when the quays at Stornoway were extended and the port generally improved. In 1554 the Old Castle defied the artillery of the Earl of Argyll, and early in the sixteenth century it held out against the "Gentleman Adventurer" from Fife. Finally it fell, but not without glory, to the MacKenzies, when they succeeded in dispossessing the old MacLeods of Lewis. The present Lewis Castle was presented to the town of Stornoway by Lord Leverhulme.

ISLAY AND JURA

ISLAY, southernmost of the Inner Hebrides, has a history as stirring and turbulent as that of any of the Scottish isles. On a rocky promontory on the south coast of the island stands Dunyveg Castle (*above*), once occupied by the Lords of the Isles. It figured prominently throughout the feud between the MacDonalds of Islay and the Macleans of Duart. Below is seen the pier at Craighouse, in Jura. The name Jura means Deer Forest, and even today Jura remains largely a deer preserve. The island's loftiest peaks, the Paps of Jura, rise in beautiful contours to a height of well over 2,000 feet, and constitute an easily recognized landmark for seamen. In olden times the island was noted for the longevity of its inhabitants.

STAFFA AND IONA

No PLACE in Christendom is more sacred to the Scots than the Isle of Iona, off the west coast of Mull. To it St. Columba came in 563 to Christianize northern Britain. The island possesses a fine abbey, the church of which has been restored and is used by the islanders for public worship. In the adjacent cemetery stand the ruins of St. Oran's Chapel (at right of picture below), the island's most ancient structure. Six miles north of Iona is the uninhabited island of Staffa, famed for its basaltic columns and great caves. The largest of the latter is Fingal's Cave, which is 227 feet. long, 42 feet wide, and 66 feet high. It was Fingal's Cave that inspired Mendelssohn to write his well-known overture, after a visit to Staffa in 1829.

BRITAIN'S HIGHEST MOUNTAIN

BEN NEVIS (4,406 ft.) is not merely the highest mountain in Scotland; it is the highest in the British Isles. Its steep northern corries afford adventurous climbing, and on some of them the snow lies all the year round. The view from the top on a clear day is that of a panorama no less than 150 miles in diameter. The flat summit may be reached without danger, except by those so sure of foot and sound of lung that they prefer to ascend by one of the more

THE BRIDLE-PATH TO THE SUMMIT

hazardous routes. That running up the flank of Glen Nevis, seen in the picture above, presents no difficulty, even to the untrained mountaineer, though he must not overlook the possibility of mists. This ascent was robbed of much of its glamour when, in the 1920's, a car, driven by a member of a well-known Edinburgh firm of motor-dealers, reached the summit. The easiest ascent is from Achintee Farm, two and a half miles from Fort William.

45

LOCH NEVIS AND LOCH HOURN

Loch Nevis (*above*), lying in the Glenelg parish of Inverness-shire, separates North Morar from Knoydart, that remote and mountainous province of the Western Highlands included in olden times in what were referred to as the Rough Bounds of Scotland. The loch itself is screened by mountains rising majestically from its shores, and clothed to a fair altitude by woodlands. Loch Nevis is said to signify "Loch of Heaven." A little farther north lies Loch Hourn (*below*). It opens from the Sound of Sleat and penetrates south-eastward, for a distance of fourteen miles, to Kinloch Hourn, the merest hamlet at its inmost reach. Its aspect of gloom, and even horror, under certain conditions is said to have earned for it a name said to mean "Loch of Hell." Its shores are sparsely populated, though the village of Arnisdale, on the north shore, in the shadow of Ben Screel, has a hundred inhabitants.

GLEN FESHIE, INVERNESS-SHIRE

HIGH up in the Grampians rises the River Feshie, a rapid stream flowing northward for twenty-three miles through the picturesque glen of the same name to join the Spey at Kincraig. A rise of barely fifty feet separates it at its source from the Geldie Burn, less than a quarter of a mile distant. This rise constitutes the water-parting of the Spey, on the one hand, and the Dee, on the other. The glen was the scene of a great flood in August, 1829.

47

LOCH AFFRIC AND THE SNOW-CAPPED RIDGE OF MAM SODHAIL

LOW TIDE AT QUEENSFERRY

ON THE southern shore of the Firth of Forth, not far from Edinburgh, and almost under the southern approach of the Forth Bridge, lies the little royal burgh of Queensferry. The town's history goes back to ancient times, certainly to the days of King Malcolm Canmore, whose queen, the saintly Margaret, so often crossed the firth here, when journeying between Edinburgh and Dunfermline, that the spot came to be known as the Queen's Ferry.

Southern Scotland

I F WE take the line between the Firth of Forth and Firth of Clyde, the part of
Scotland south of it is a definite entity, the Lowlands of general speech. The
line divides the Central Plain of the geographer, the wide vale in which is placed
the greater part of Scotland's heavy industry. Here in the Lothians, in Lanarkshire and North Ayrshire are coal mines in plenty, a fair number of shale oil
mines and some ironworks. The shale bings rise black and pink and detract from
the fair country, and chimneys belch in the manner of chimneys, yet in Scotland
there has never arisen quite that seeming sterilization of nature which one feels in
the Lancashire-Yorkshire industrial conurbation. I can think of no Lanarkshire
hill, or Renfrew or Dumbarton hill above the Clyde, as being anywhere near as
dirty and the sheep so black as on the poor Pennines between Manchester and
Sheffield. The countryside of Scotland comes near, keeps near or is not pushed
back very easily from the industrialization which is no less ruthless than its English
counterpart.

Edinburgh has wild country within the City boundary and from thousands
of windows the Pentland Hills are clear to the south or the Lomond Hills of Fife
to the north. A threepenny bus gets you into pleasant country. Glasgow is even
more miraculously served, considering the enormous spread of this second city
of Britain. Loch Lomond and the Trossachs are as the northern gate, there are the
moors and little farms scarcely more than crofts around East Kilbride and Eagle-
sham, and above all the incomparable Clyde. It is not my home river and I would
not care to live at Greenock, Gourock, Helensburgh or Dunoon, but I bow to her
as the Queen of Rivers. The Firth of Clyde has an amazing capacity for holding
all these no'-so-bonnie excrescences and being none the less beautiful.

The Firth of Forth is crisper and not the kindly mother of the innocent babes
who insist on learning to sail; there is no Holy Loch and Hunter's Quay to warm
the heart. Fisherrow or Newhaven or Granton, with their gritty little harbours, are
occupied by the professionals, the inshore fishermen of the Forth, whose grand
women cry the fresh-caught food through the stone canyons of Edinburgh. The
Firth of Forth is to be looked upon with constant interest and delight; the Firth
of Clyde is to be sailed upon by everybody, even by those who would suffer elsewhere from the dreadful malaise.

Between and beyond the southern limits of these two firths lies the plinth of
Scotland as it were, the Southern Uplands of the geographer, and the Border

Country. Much of the pastoral wealth of the country is here and the home of such famous breeds of cattle and sheep as the sweet Ayrshire dairy cow, the black Galloway so important to the beef market, the Border Leicester sheep and those foundation hill breeds, the Blackface and the Cheviot. These animals are quite inseparable from the landscape. Indeed, in a large measure they have helped to make it; the sheep farming of the Southern Uplands is not more than five hundred years old. Before that time the greater part of the hills was covered with forest growth—oak, birch and pine, but the extension of sheep ranching cleared all that so that now we tend to forget it was ever there.

One of the problems of the future is to get some forest and tree cover back. The disastrous flood of the south-eastern valleys of Scotland in August, 1948, followed a precipitation of four inches of rain in a few hours; the countryside as it is was unable to soak up a large proportion of this and let it down gently into the rivers. Had the Lammermuirs been forest instead of over-grazed sheep-walk there would probably have been no disaster. Forestry and pastoralism are always in conflict, the world over, and until now pastoral interests have won too many rounds. But in southern Scotland the Forestry Commission is planting up large areas and certainly altering the landscape. The forests of Newcastleton, of Ae in Dumfriesshire and of the Roxburgh Cheviots are an inspiring sight.

The Forestry Commission has also acquired large areas in the mountainous country of Galloway, round Loch Trool and the Merrick. Much of the ground will be unplantable and the Commission is creating a National Forest Park in the area, with most painstaking care to enhance rather than detract from landscape values. It is certain that the beauties of this region will be easier seen in the future.

The quiet farming lands south of Ayr are as kind as any in England. The Old Red Sandstone and the western sea create perfect conditions for early potatoes and the fields are truly a picture. The coal measures have been left behind and man's influence has been in general to make the landscape kind rather than to despoil. South of Girvan again are hosts of small upland farms and soon you are over the watershed into the Stewartry, another green country of dairy farms where the red and white cattle stand out sharp on the pastures. The Isle of Whithorn is near the southern tip of Burrow Head, a true isle no more, but the place of St. Ninian's Kirk, where Christianity was first brought to Scotland, and the site of *Candida Casa*, from which there was so much missionary activity.

This very brief review could scarcely close without mention of the Valley of the Tweed from Melrose to below Kelso. It is a favoured land of low ground backed by easy hills and the farms are well done. It is the country of the great abbeys of Melrose and Dryburgh, rather than of the harder one of Border keeps not so far away. A few miles below Kelso, at Carham, England breaks in to claim the south bank of the Tweed and from there the spell of Scotland seems broken.

KELSO ABBEY, ROXBURGHSHIRE

KELSO ABBEY was founded by King David I in 1128. Today little remains of it but the walls of the north and north-west transepts, the Galilee porch, part of the western tower, and a few isolated pillars. The monks of Kelso, in common with their brethren at the other Border abbeys, fought valiantly against the English invaders who, from time to time, ravaged the Borderland with fire and sword, laying waste its sacred places. All the Border abbeys were pillaged and burnt during the sixteenth century.

THE SCOTT COUNTRY

ARCHITECTURALLY, KELSO is famous among the towns of Britain. Its square is an unrivalled example of early planning, and the fine five-arch bridge across the Tweed, erected by Rennie, was the first bridge with the elliptic arch. Its architect took it as his model for the Old Waterloo Bridge. On the right bank of the Tweed, about two miles west of Melrose, stands Abbotsford (*below*), the huge baronial pile which Sir Walter Scott erected between 1817 and 1821, and where he died in 1832. Here one may still see his immense library and many of his intimate possessions. The most prominent landmark in the Scott Country is the three summits known as the Eildons (*below, right*). This group of hills, standing apart, has a striking appearance from all sides. Popular tradition presents them as originally one mountain cleft in three by the magic wand of the wizard, Michael Scott. The country on every side is rich in history and legend. This is the land of Border feuds and forays, Border battles and ballads. A stone on the slope of the north-eastern hill marks the spot where stood the Eildon Tree, under which Thomas the Rhymer, the thirteenth-century Scottish poet, confided to the credulous his doleful prophecies.

THE ANNAN AND CLUDEN WATER

DUMFRIESSHIRE'S principal rivers, the Annan (seen below at Brydekirk) and the Nith, linger through country which is rich in literary associations. With Dumfries one instantly associates the name of Robert Burns, who died there in 1796; with Maxwelltown, that of Annie Laurie; with Ecclefechan, that of Thomas Carlyle; with Caerlaverock, that of Sir Walter Scott's *Ellangowan*. In the churchyard at Caerlaverock stands a monument to Robert Paterson, the "Old Mortality" of Scott's novel of that name. Roughly a mile and a half to the north-west of Dumfries, the Cluden Water falls into the Nith close to Lincluden Abbey (*left*). This ruined religious house, founded in the twelfth century, was used originally as a convent for Benedictine nuns, but was later turned into a collegiate church. It was one of Burns's favourite haunts.

EYEMOUTH AND DRYBURGH ABBEY

A FEW miles north of Berwick-upon-Tweed stands the little fishing town of Eyemouth. In olden times its harbour was a favourite haunt of smugglers, and many of its ancient dwelling-houses still boast the deep cellars in which contraband goods were stored. Fishing has been prosecuted at Eyemouth from earliest times, and the oldest inhabitants still recall the great disaster of 1881 when 129 of its fishermen lost their lives in a terrific gale which halved the port's fishing fleet. Dryburgh is one of the four famous abbeys of the Borderland for which King David I, youngest son of King Malcolm Canmore, was responsible. Melrose, Kelso, and Jedburgh are the others. In its only remaining aisle Sir Walter Scott is buried, and close at hand is the tomb of Earl Haig.

ST. MARY'S LOCH, SELKIRKSHIRE

ON THE border between Selkirk and Peebles lies St. Mary's Loch, a lovely and romantic sheet of water no more than three miles in length and but half a mile at its maximum width. No loch in Lowland Scotland has found its way more frequently into literature. In *Marmion* Scott paints a perfect picture of its setting, while Wordsworth did not omit to record its beauties. More intimately associated with it, however, is the name of James Hogg, the Ettrick Shepherd, whose monument stands at the head of the loch.

TRAQUAIR HOUSE, PEEBLESSHIRE

TRAQUAIR HOUSE, parts of which are said to be at least 950 years old, stands in the Quair
Valley, hard by the Tweed. This ancient domicile, built in the style of the old château, has
been added to from time to time, chiefly during the reign of Charles I. The old gateway
is believed to have suggested to Scott his description of Tully Veolan in *Waverley*. The
avenue leading up to this gateway has not been used since 1796, when the seventh Earl of
Traquair closed the gates after the death of his countess. However, as the Traquairs were
fervent Jacobites, local tradition has it that they were shut with the downfall of the House
of Stuart, never to be re-opened until a Stuart returned to the throne.

KIRKCUDBRIGHT: THE CASTLE AND GRANARIES, FROM THE RIVER DEE

A COUNTY OF CONTRASTS

WIGTOWNSHIRE is a combination of rugged grandeur on the one hand, and of arcadian beauty on the other. The Mull of Galloway, the tip of which forms the southernmost part of Scotland, is a fourteen-mile extension of the county into the North Channel. Its cliffy coastline, seen above at West Tarbet Bay, is of an average height of 200 feet. In contrast with the rugged scenery of the Mull is Newton Stewart (*below*). This charming little town, standing on the River Cree, where it is spanned by a five-arch granite bridge, derives its name from William Stewart, third son of the second Earl of Galloway, who built many of its houses. In the Inch parish of Wigtownshire stand the village, lake, and ruined mansion-house of Castle Kennedy. The last, seen at left, was built by the fifth Earl of Cassilis in 1607. Seventy years later it passed, together with the surrounding property, to Sir John Dalrymple, later Earl of Stair. It was destroyed by fire in 1716 and was never restored.

MOSSGIEL, NEAR MAUCHLINE

FEW places are more intimately associated with the life and works of Robert Burns than is the Ayrshire town of Mauchline. Its old church was the scene of his *Holy Fair*, and in its graveyard may be seen the tombstones of Mary Morison, Holy Willie, Daddy Auld, and others whom he immortalized. Less than a mile from Mauchline is Mossgiel, the farm of 118 acres which Burns and his brother, Gilbert, tenanted from 1784 until 1788, and where Robert wrote many of his most famous verses.

BRIG O' DOON

"NAIBODY sings the Doon," Burns complained in 1785, and then proceeded to rectify the omission in his song *Ye Banks and Braes o' Bonnie Doon.* On the right bank of the Doon, but two miles south of Ayr, stands the little town of Alloway, where Burns was born in 1759. Alloway's auld, haunted kirk is the scene of Tam o' Shanter's memorable encounter with the wraith. Hard by the Burns monument at Alloway, the Auld Brig o' Doon spans the river for ever associated with him.

THE VILLAGE OF CROSSFORD, LANARKSHIRE

FEW associate the Clyde with anything except shipping and the heavy industries, yet the upper reaches of the valley through which flows this historic river are covered with orchards presenting in springtime a spectacle as arcadian as may be seen at that season of the year in Kent or in the Vale of Evesham. The village of Crossford lies in the heart of this northern orchardland. At the neighbouring town of Carluke much of the fruit grown in the Clyde valley is used commercially for jam-making.

EARLY SOCIAL EXPERIMENT

STANDING on low ground by the banks of the Clyde, but a mile from Lanark proper, is the large manufacturing centre of New Lanark, founded in 1783 by the enterprising and philanthropic David Dale as a seat of cotton manufacture. From the end of the eighteenth century until 1827 it was the model scene of the social experiments made by Robert Owen, Dale's son-in-law. This well-built village afforded to the employees many of the attractions so singularly absent from the industrial centres of the period. The first mill was opened there in 1785, and during the succeeding decade as many as four were in a flourishing condition. Each mill was constructed to the same plan.

TWO CLYDE LANDMARKS

THE busy industrial town of Dumbarton offers many fine prospects of mountain, river, and estuary, but few so intimate as that from the Rock. Dumbarton Rock, like Ailsa Craig, is of granite, and is one of the Clyde's best-known landmarks. In olden times it was fortified and had a governor. Another well-known landmark is the Cloch Lighthouse (seen at left from the Cowal coast), built in 1797 on a small peninsula of Renfrewshire known as Cloch Point. Between this point and Dunoon the Firth is at its narrowest. Scottish sailors and passengers alike regard it as something with a definite significance. When outward-bound, the passing of the Cloch means that one has now turned south into the Firth of Clyde proper, leaving home behind, as it were. Inward-bound, it denotes that the oceanic part of one's voyage is over and that one has arrived once more in home waters.

THE BONNIE, BONNIE BANKS

THIS photograph of Loch Lomond and the famous Ben (3,192 feet) is taken looking towards Craigroyston, in the Stirlingshire parish of Buchanan, on the east side of the loch. Here is the famous cavern known as Rob Roy's Cave, which lies within a steep, rugged rock a little above the water's edge, its narrow entrance largely concealed by fallen boulders. Robert the Bruce spent a night here after the skirmish at Dalry in 1306. Four centuries or so later it was to become a hiding-place of the freebooter and outlaw, Rob Roy MacGregor.

PASSENGERS DISEMBARKING AT LUSS

THE Dunbartonshire village of Luss, by the western shores of Loch Lomond, is one of Scotland's model villages. At any time of the year it is orderly and beautiful. It should be seen, however, in high summer or in autumn, when its cottage gardens are a riot of aspiring colour. One would imagine in autumn that its cottagers vied with one another in the display of phloxes. At Luss pier the steamers call in their passages up and down this remarkable lake, often disembarking scores of tourists intent on exploring the Bonnie, Bonnie Banks.

STIRLING CASTLE

STIRLING CASTLE, perched on a rock commanding the surrounding plain, through which the River Forth winds slowly and broadly, is a place of historic significance as important as that of any ancient stronghold in Scotland. In 1296 it was occupied by the troops of Edward I, that veritable Hammer o' the Scots. The following year Sir William Wallace recaptured it after the Battle of Stirling Bridge. The Castle was a favourite residence of the Stuart monarchs. Here James II of Scotland was born in 1430, and in the chamber known as the Douglas Room he assassinated the young Earl of Douglas for his treasonable conduct in 1452. Subsequent Jameses all had intimate connexions with this ancient fortress which, in 1746, successfully resisted Prince Charlie's army.

HOLYROOD PALACE

OVERSHADOWED by Arthur's Seat, at the foot of Edinburgh's Royal Mile, stands Holyrood, consisting of an ancient Abbey and a Royal Palace. The Palace, as distinct from the Abbey, was founded by James IV in 1501. In 1543 it was mostly destroyed by English forces under Hertford, but was afterwards rebuilt on a more splendid scale. The most critical event in Holyrood's history was the murder of David Rizzio in 1566. The apartments occupied by Mary Queen of Scots are a source of constant interest to the thousands who flock to Holyrood every year, there to be shown not only Mary's bed, but also some dark stains on the stairs said to be those of the blood of the murdered Rizzio.

PRINCES STREET, EDINBURGH

THE BASS ROCK FROM THE RUINS OF TANTALLON CASTLE

STANDING at the mouth of the Firth of Forth, but one and a quarter miles from the East Lothian coast, is the rocky islet known as the Bass. This conspicuous landmark carries a lighthouse, and on its surface of seven acres sheep are pastured. On its cliffs the solan goose breeds in great numbers. The islet first appears on record as the hermitage of St. Baldred, founder of Tyningham monastery, who died on it in 756. The ruins of an ancient chapel upon it are believed to occupy the site of the saint's cell.

COWSLIPS BY THE EAST LOTHIAN SHORE

EAST LOTHIAN is a maritime county with a coastline of thirty-two miles, half of which lies along the Firth of Forth. The climate of the coastal parts is usually mild, as is shown by the profusion of wild flowers quite early in springtime. The soil is remarkably productive, and rich loam is plentiful. Here are grown the famous potatoes known as Dunbar Reds. The natural advantages of soil and climate, together with the skill of the farmers and farm-workers, are almost sufficient to account for the country's great agricultural prosperity.

THE FORTH BRIDGE FROM DALMENY, NEAR EDINBURGH

IN THE HEART OF THE TROSSACHS

THE beauties of Loch Achray, in south-western Perthshire, have been sung by innumerable poets and travellers. *The Lady of the Lake* thoroughly acquainted the world with the glories of this corner of the Central Highlands, so sweet and lovely in its "copsewood grey." Yet Coleridge and the Wordsworths had already ensured for it a permanent place in literature. On its northern shore stand a little church, a manse, and the castellated Trossachs Hotel, seen above, where Nathaniel Hawthorne sojourned in 1857.

The East
of Scotland

THE country between the Firth of Forth and the Moray Firth is peopled by a predominantly Norse stock. The dialects spoken are quite different from the Saxon derivatives of the Border and Ayrshire; the domestic architecture is often different also, whitewashed houses of the south-west and the dwelling-cum-byre of Ayrshire giving way to buildings in stone, crow-stepped gables and a surprising number of fine old houses of the fortified period. I would say you would find more interesting Scots building between Forth and Moray than can be found in the same area elsewhere in Scotland.

Fife itself is full of good architecture from medieval to Georgian times—Culross, Falkland, the fishing villages of St. Monance and Anstruther and so on. Unfortunately, the presence of coal, which should be a blessing, has also caused the creation of Lochgelly and Cowdenbeath. Fife away from the collieries is a rich agricultural county, and now that the East Fife coalfield is to be exploited we can only hope that new colliery towns will not ruin the Fair Kingdom.

The Firth of Tay, where Fife and Angus look across at each other, is the gateway of what, to a naturalist, is the heart of Scotland. It is a shallow firth with seal-inhabited sandbanks dry at low tides. Those sandbanks are indicative: a large part of the great Tay Basin is composed of that excellent rock Old Red Sandstone, which breaks down easily and washes away all too readily. Also, the Tay comes roaring down out of the Highlands through an area of much glacial drift and through some of the shattered formations of the Highland Border Fault; so the river is always carrying down sand and shingle, and along its course from Aberfeldy to the sea it is a water of many shingle islands and grassed-over islands of alluvium.

This kind of river is just right for salmon, and the fishery is an important factor in the prosperity of the area. And the flats make the mouth of the river a resting ground for the wild geese of the east of Scotland. The disposition of Loch Leven in Kinross, the resting grounds of the Tay and the sandy peninsulas to seaward make this area supremely important to the migrant waterfowl.

The long stretch of Old Red Sandstone reaching from the Firth of Clyde to Stonehaven, and thus passing through the Tay Basin, holds some of the best-farmed land in Scotland. The prices of farms in the best of this, as around Arbroath, compare with the highest in Britain. Such land in the hands of a practical people tends to limit hedges, hedgerow trees and woods, but I know this opinion of a tendency to bareness would be hotly disputed by a people very proud of their good land. And it is far from being true for the south-western end round Callander and Doune, and of parts of Strath More. The little towns of this great farming region reflect the energy and marketing power of the people. They are packed with goods and are as Aladdin's caves to one who has passed a long time in the west.

Had we followed up the Tay we should have come to Perth itself, a town and countryside of much grace. Grace is the right word for much of Perthshire. The land is not quite so good as in that eastern stretch, it is more varied in contour, and, whether you like it or not, there is nothing like having a duke in the neighbourhood for making country look its best. When you reach Dunkeld you are in the domains of the Duke of Atholl, and for well over two hundred years the Dukes have been devotees of forestry and good trees. Even now, after the devastations of two wars and crippling taxation, the Atholl Estates are a picture of good forestry and everywhere there is a wealth of trees for the sake of amenity. The influence of Atholl must have been considerable elsewhere in Perthshire in these two hundred years, for there is no county in Scotland with better plantations to show or more specimen trees, and there are natural advantages tending to keep trees, for example, the deep, oak-bedecked gorge of Killiecrankie, and the many little hills composed of glacial drift which are too poor and dry for agricultural use.

The diamond-shaped county of Aberdeen occupies the extremity of the eastern peninsula of Scotland on the south shore of the Moray Firth, and reaches back into the Cairngorms to the highest hills there, of Ben Macdhui (4,296 feet), Braeriach (4,248 feet) and Cairn Toul (4,241 feet). Within Aberdeenshire is a great range of conditions. This landward point of the diamond is given up to deer forests and forestry, amid truly magnificent scenery. And up here in the very tip rises the River Dee, which swells into a noble torrent by the time it reaches Braemar. Balmoral is built on its banks and on it flows through a beautiful valley until it reaches the sea at Aberdeen. The other great river of Aberdeenshire is the Don, coming south-eastwards from good farming land to the sea just north of Aberdeen.

The plough goes far in Aberdeenshire. It stops climbing only when the land ceases to yield. A journey through the Garioch takes one through a constantly toughening terrain, until in the Glens of Foudland small bare farms are still running mainly as arable above the 1,000-foot contour.

Down in Moray, the country all round Elgin, the scene and climate have changed to kindliness. This is the sunniest strip of Scotland and the driest. Fochabers, Elgin, Forres, these are towns with Georgian ancestry and earlier. The ruined cathedral at Elgin and the abbey at Pluscarden show the level of civilization this area had reached five hundred years ago.

BLAIR CASTLE, PERTHSHIRE

LESS than a mile from the Perthshire village of Blair-Atholl stands Blair Castle, seat of the Duke of Atholl, and one of the most historic houses in Scotland. As restored about 1872, it consists of a fine, four-storeyed mansion, with turrets and battlements in Scots baronial style. Comyn's Tower, its oldest part, is said to have been built by John de Strathbogie, ninth Earl of Atholl, in the thirteenth century. It was here that, in 1644, Montrose mustered the four thousand Atholl Highlanders whom he led to victory at Tippermuir. In 1653 the castle was stormed and destroyed by Colonel Daniel, one of Cromwell's officers. Yet, in 1689, we find it garrisoned by Claverhouse, whose body, brought back to it after the Battle of Killiecrankie, was buried in the old church of Blair.

85

THE TAY BRIDGE FROM THE AIR

THE Firth of Tay is spanned between Angus and Fife by a railway viaduct opened in 1888 to replace the earlier bridge destroyed by storm in 1879. It is one of the world's longest bridges, being over two miles in length. A little to the east of it may be seen the piers of the old bridge, all the high central girders of which, on the evening of Sunday, 28 December, 1879, were blown down while a northbound passenger train was crossing it. Every individual on that ill-fated train perished. A protracted inquiry established that the bridge had been badly designed, badly built, and badly maintained. The Tay Bridge Disaster is always listed as one of Scotland's major calamities.

LOCH KATRINE AND THE CITY OF PERTH

LOCH KATRINE is one of Scotland's loveliest and most romantic freshwater lochs. The famed Trossachs are situated at one end of it, and Glen Gyle, birthplace of Rob Roy MacGregor, at the other. The loch and its environs are the scene of Scott's *The Lady of the Lake*. Loch Katrine supplies the greater part of Glasgow with water, and the several occasions upon which its level has had to be raised, in order to increase its volume for this purpose, have submerged much of its beauty, and many a site famed in legend, literature, and song. Perth, seen below from Kinnoull Hill, is one of the oldest and most historic cities in the land. It stands on the River Tay, at the foot of Strathtay and the head of the fertile Carse of Gowrie. In situation and appearance, as well as in the colour of its history and the temperament of its inhabitants, it has been likened to Paris.

THE BRAES OF BALQUHIDDER

Few places in Scotland are better known than Balquhidder. In the graveyard surrounding the ivy-mantled ruins of the old kirk, on the celebrated Braes of Balquhidder, are three recumbent stones marking the burial-place of Rob Roy, of Helen MacGregor, his wife, and one of their sons. For many years the MacLaurins were the most powerful clan in this region. Tradition says that they occupied it in the ninth century, during the reign of Kenneth MacAlpin, first King of Scots. In 1588, however, the chief of the clan, together with his aged and infirm adherents, was massacred by a band of incendiarists from Glendochart. The murderers are believed to have been MacGregors who, for years past, had been their greatest enemies. A monument in the churchyard commemorates this event,

THE MERCAT CROSS AND SQUARE, CULROSS, FIFE

THE history of Culross is a cross-section of that of Scotland from earliest times. Here, in A.D. 424, St. Palladius, while on a mission from Rome to convert the Scots, found St. Serf already established. Until a hundred years ago Culross was a place of some importance. Indeed, in the manufacture of girdles, in which James VI granted it a monopoly, it had no rival. The preservation of Culross has been a special feature of the activities of the National Trust for Scotland since its inception. The Trust holds more than a score of separate properties in this ancient Royal Burgh. They consist of typical Scots houses of the late sixteenth and early seventeenth centuries, and include Sir George Bruce's famous Palace, later called "the Colonel's Close," and the celebrated "Study" of Bishop Leighton, seen below.

A GLIMPSE INTO FIFE

IN THE East Neuk of Fife lies the little seaport of Crail, seen above, which figured early in the ninth century as a centre of commerce with the Netherlands and as one of the most important fish and fish-curing stations on the east coast of Scotland. Fishing is still carried on, but in recent years it has become better known as a holiday resort. Dunfermline Abbey (*left*) was, at the close of the thirteenth century, one of the most extensive and magnificent monastic establishments in Scotland. Early in the fourteenth century it was occupied by Edward I of England, who fired it and otherwise damaged it, but it was restored when Scotland became more settled under Robert the Bruce.

ELGIN AND THE SPEY

THE crowning glory of Moray, a region rich in archaeological interest, is Elgin Cathedral (*right*), often referred to in the annals of Scotland as the Lantern of the North. The hand of the destroyer has fallen on it often, but never so heavily as did that of Alexander Stewart, Earl of Buchan, better known to Scottish history as the Wolf of Badenoch. Excommunicated for having seized some Church lands, he descended in wrath on Moray in 1390 and, after burning the town of Forres, burned Elgin and its cathedral. The ruins as seen today are much as the Wolf's sacrilege left them. The River Spey, seen below at Fochabers, is Scotland's most rapid river. Although of no commercial importance, in point of length and volume of water, it is inferior only to the Tay and the Tweed.

THE CULBIN SANDS, MORAY

THE Culbin Sands, bounded on the north and west by the sandy shores of the Moray
Firth, are the only region in Britain where sand-dunes and shifting sandhills occupy an
area sufficiently large to create the impression that they compose a lifeless, arid desert. In
1921 the Forestry Commission began to acquire land at Culbin, where it now owns roughly
5,500 acres. The following year the Commission began planting pine-trees, with the result
that a considerable area of what formerly was desert has been reclaimed.

RIVER DEVERON, FROM BRIDGE OF ALVAH

AT BRIDGE OF ALVAH, two miles south of Banff, a quaint bridge crosses the Deveron, a river shared by the counties of Aberdeen and Banff. It rises among the Cabrach mountains in two main head-streams; hence the Gaelic origin of its name—"double river." Its connexions with the two counties are, indeed, fitful. At one moment it flows into the one; at another it flows into the other; at yet another it forms the boundary between the two. It reaches the sea eventually between Banff and the somewhat smaller town of Macduff.

THE DIVERSITY OF BANFF

AGRICULTURE and fishing are the two main industries of Banff. Its seaboard, fringing the Moray Firth, is almost solely dependent upon the herring fishings, the centre of which industry is Buckie, a port from which drifters, manned by crews from the town itself, or from the several fisher-folk communities in its neighbourhood, operate throughout the season. The fishing village of Portgordon, seen above, also does a flourishing trade in salmon. Loch Avon (*left*), with the exception of Loch Einich, is the largest of the sheets of fresh water enfolded by the Cairngorm mountains. It lies in the northern part of them, with peaks on every side, loftiest of them Cairn Gorm itself, rising to a height of 4,084 feet.

94

BALMORAL CASTLE, ABERDEENSHIRE

ON THE south bank of the River Dee, in the parish of Crathie, stands the royal residence of Balmoral. The estate was purchased in 1848 by Prince Albert, who presented it to Queen Victoria. The foundation-stone of the present building was laid in September, 1853, and it was not quite finished when the Royal Family entered it just two years later. An earlier pile, occupied throughout several seasons by the Royal Family, stood on adjoining ground.

THE CAIRNGORMS, FROM NEAR BRAEMAR, ABERDEENSHIRE

BRAEMAR, ABERDEENSHIRE

NEW Braemar Castle (*seen above*) stands near the ruins of an older castle which is said to have been a hunting seat of King Malcolm Canmore. Later it became a stronghold of the Earls of Mar. The new castle was built about 1720 by parties who had acquired the estates forfeited by the eleventh Earl of Mar because of his Jacobite activities. Incidentally, it was he who, in 1715, raised the standard for the Old Chevalier on the Braes of Mar. Today Braemar is famous chiefly for its annual Gathering, said to have originated in an unpremeditated display of athletic prowess during a boat hunt in Malcolm Canmore's time. Perhaps its principal attraction is the Highland Games (*seen below*), at which proficiency in every form of athleticism is demonstrated, including the ancient Highland sport of "tossing the caber." Piping and dancing competitions remain two of the major features of this annual event.

THE SUMMIT CLIFFS OF LOCHNAGAR

THE granite mountain of Lochnagar rises to a height of 3,786 ft. above sea-level in the Braemar region of Aberdeenshire. Its flanks, for the most part, are so steep as to be scalable on foot only with the expenditure of much energy. Yet, in September, 1848, Queen Victoria and the Prince Consort reached the summit on sturdy Highland ponies. Byron, who described Lochnagar as "the most sublime and picturesque of the Caledonian Alps," celebrated its steep, frowning glories in one of the best known of his minor poems.

ABERDEEN AND THE RIVER DEE

ABERDEEN stands between the rivers Dee and Don, and is the most important seaport in the north of Scotland. From earliest times it has been a fishing port of considerable significance, and in the height of the season its spacious harbour is astir with all manner of fishing craft. The University, founded in 1494, has long been the seat at which Highland students have graduated, while its Agricultural College is the best known of its kind in the United Kingdom. The country through which the Dee flows before entering the sea at Aberdeen is famous for its scenery. The river rises in the very heart of the Cairngorms, and the steepness of its fall in several places provides it with a velocity which can indeed be spectacular, especially after a heavy rainfall. But, except in time of spate, its quieter stretches, such as that near Balmoral (*below*), are peaceful and pastoral. Nowhere has the Dee in tumult wrought more havoc than in the vicinity of Ballater (*below, left*). Here the river is spanned by a fine four-arched bridge, erected more than a century ago to replace at least two predecessors which had been swept away by floods.

THE HARBOUR AT STONEHAVEN, KINCARDINE

DUNNOTTAR CASTLE, KINCARDINE

CROWNING the flat summit of an enormous rock not far from Stonehaven is Dunnottar, a ruined fortress all but separated from the mainland by a chasm. The earliest stronghold on this site was built in the seventh century. The castle of later days was occupied by the Keiths, Earls Marischal of Scotland. During the reigns of Charles II and James VII, Dunnottar became a state prison in which Covenanters were immured and tormented.

GLAMIS CASTLE AND GLEN ISLA, ANGUS

GLAMIS CASTLE, seat of the Earl of Strathmore and Kinghorne, consists in its present form mainly of reconstructions and additions of the sixteenth and seventeenth centuries, though tradition ascribes its earliest foundations to the tenth. It is considered to be one of the finest examples of the Scottish Baronial style of architecture. The Castle, which houses one of the best-known ghosts in Scotland, is said to have been the scene of the murder of Malcolm II, in 1034. In north-west Angus is the parish of Glen Isla, containing the lovely glen of the same name, seen below. The whole area is one of great beauty, especially where the River Isla falls at the cataracts known as the Reekie Linn and the Slugs of Achrannie.

LEAVING KYLE OF LOCHALSH

KYLE OF LOCHALSH, in Wester Ross, consisted of the merest handful of thatched cottages until the opening of the Dingwall-Skye Railway toward the close of the last century, when it became its western terminus. It is situated within a few hundred yards of Kyleakin, in Skye itself, and is one of the three railheads in the Western Highlands from which the Hebrides are reached by a regular mail-boat service.

The Far North

WE ARE in the farthest lands of Scotland, and it is almost impossible not to feel this anywhere in these wide territories except, perhaps, in Kirkwall, capital of a thriving agricultural county. But there is still something different from the rest of Scotland, perhaps because Kirkwall is the heritor of a pure Norse kingdom, one that lasted for six hundred years and was not absorbed into the realm of Scotland until 1469. So, too, with Shetland, that other Norse outpost, but Kirkwall was like the centre of an empire with Shetland and the Outer Hebrides as dominions, trading with the northern and western world. The prosperity and vigour of Orkney are no new things. Then, as now, there were the facts of many and excellent harbours and of the land being Old Red Sandstone. It is the stuff of good farms. The climate is windy, but only half as wet or less than half as on the West Highland coast. Orkney still shows that light-hearted quality in living which is common to the Scandinavian countries. The trials of a suffering Britain seem less imminent in these gay and thriving islands.

Shetland is more like the Outer Hebrides. The land is generally poor and crofting preponderates over farming. The men are at sea or follow the fishing, just as in Lewis, and the magnificent women of both archipelagos do a great deal of the work of the croft. Lerwick is an older town than Stornoway and breathes the fact, somehow, but the two have much in common, with their visiting seasonal fishing fleets and a frontier quality they can never dispel. Kirkwall of Orkney is not concerned today with more than domestic fishing and the town is for the towns-folk and the farmers of Orkney. Lerwick and Stornoway are for the wider world today. Lerwick is only a hundred miles from Bergen.

In these few words of introduction to the far north it is surely permissible to take in the outliers of the Hebrides and of Orkney and Shetland to speak of the wealth of wild life which is to be found in the small, remote islands of this far region. There should be a special map, so projected as to show the wondrous chain of the little isles. Start at St. Kilda, forty miles west of North Uist, an island group unique in the North Atlantic in the gaunt, terrific nature of its scenery, and unique as the largest gannetry in the world. The sum total of other sea-birds making it a metropolis must be millions. Then the seven Flannan Isles, seventeen miles west of Gallan Head in Lewis, awe-inspiring when it comes to landing on them; Sula Sgeir, thirty-three miles north-east of the Butt of Lewis, a great rough rock crowned with gannets and defeating many an attempt at landing; North

Rona, an emerald of the northern ocean, forty-seven miles north-west of Cape Wrath and ninety miles west of Orkney, and the home of the largest stock of Atlantic seals in the world; Sule Stack, thirty miles north of Loch Eriboll, a mere six acres and 125 feet high, looking like a great sailing yacht when the gannets whiten it; Sule Skerry, a few miles north-east of Sule Stack, a flat expanse of rock where Atlantic seals lived until the lighthouse came; Foula, the great outlier of Shetland, vieing with St. Kilda for the highest sheer sea-cliff in Britain; Muckle Flugga, the northernmost point of the British Isles, very wild, very majestic, bearing a lighthouse and a recently established gannetry. This is the array we should remember when apt to be overawed by pictures of the big game of Africa or the wild life of the North American national parks.

The mainland of the far north is equally a wonderland in its different way. This time no wastes of seas, but wastes of land among the hills. The mountain scenery of this region differs from that farther south in that the hills tend to be more isolated among the vast areas of broken bog. There is the superb Foinaven range in the farthest north-west, well separated from the fine shapes of Ben Hope, Ben Loyal and Ben Clibreck, the great hills near the north coast. South again, the traveller comes into the fantastic country of the Torridonian sandstone and rock-bun hills of Archaean gneiss. There is nothing else in Scotland like Suilven and Stac Polly, fairy castles the colour of wine as the sun goes down. Their isolation is enhancing to their splendour, but still farther south are the great massifs of the Teallach and the Torridonian ranges, rising to almost three thousand five hundred feet and exceedingly spiry. There is more sky-room among these hills than farther south in the Highlands and the photographer has magnificent opportunities. This is the remote land of great deer forests and of golden eagles; of short, rushing rivers of high rental for the salmon fishing; and, above all, of a great peace and quietness.

The central moors of Sutherland, at the head of Strath Naver and Strath Halladale and over to Loch Choire, are quite the vastest and most sublime in restful line of any in the kingdom—mile after mile after mile, and very still when the wind is quiet. This is the great sheep country of the North, very sparsely inhabited but very important to the farming of the rest of Scotland, for the lambs from the prodigious sales at Lairg go far and wide to the low country.

Caithness finishes this wonderful country of the far north and in its way it is no tamer than the mountainous land farther west. It is a vast undulating plain of Old Red Sandstone, covered in many places by deep peat bogs. Certainly there are trees in Caithness, but they have to be hunted. This great plain between the northern ocean and the eastern sea is the home of every wind that blows and the stranger rarely finds it quiet. The architecture of the little farm steadings is distinctive and pleasing and in keeping with a country of the winds. In Caithness the eye rests afar.

LOCH TORRIDON, WESTER ROSS

LOCH TORRIDON, one of the most splendid sea-lochs in Scotland, is situated in the Apple-cross parish of Wester Ross. At its entrance it measures four and a half miles, contracts near Shieldaig to three furlongs, and thereafter attains, in Upper Loch Torridon, a width of nearly two miles. Bold, precipitous mountains surround it, the loftiest of which are Liathach (3,456 feet) and Ben Alligin (3,232 feet). At the head of the loch is the tiny clachan of Torridon, with its inn and post office.

LOCH DUICH, ROSS-SHIRE

IN THAT part of Wester Ross known as Kintail lies Loch Duich, undoubtedly one of the loveliest and most romantic settings in the Highlands. It runs inland almost to the base of that fine range of peaks known as the Five Sisters of Kintail, which, together with much of the adjoining moorland country, is now the property of the National Trust for Scotland. On an islet at the mouth of the loch stands Eilean Donan Castle, restored in 1932 after the cannonading it received in the Jacobite uprising known as "The Nineteen."

ULLAPOOL, LOCH BROOM

In 1788 the British Fishery Society founded in the Loch Broom parish of Ross-shire the village of Ullapool in the belief that one day it would develop into a prosperous town. Through the great decline in the herring fisheries, however, this dream was never realized. Herring fishing is still prosecuted, but to no great extent. About the middle of the last century the village passed into the possession of Sir James Matheson, who improved it considerably and erected its lines of whitewashed and slated houses.

PLOCKTON, LOCH CARRON, ROSS-SHIRE

LOCH MAREE AND SLIOCH

LOCH MAREE is believed to have once formed part of Loch Ewe, the sea-loch into which it overflows. Silt and sand are thought to have dammed its lower end, thus forming a fresh-water as well as a salt-water loch—a belief supported by the fact that Kinlochewe, meaning "head of Loch Ewe," is the name of the village at the head of Loch Maree. The loch is overlooked by mountains of great height, loftiest of them being Slioch (3,217 feet) to the north-east, and Ben Eighe (3,309 feet) to the south-west. The loch derives its name from Eilean Maree, one of its large cluster of islets. On this islet stood a hermit's cell associated not with St. Mary's, as so many suppose, but with the saintly Maolrubha, the Red Priest, whose memory is enshrined in several place-names in this locality.

THE TOWN CLOCK AT TAIN, EASTER ROSS

CLOSE to the southern shore of the Dornoch Firth stands the small town of Tain. The town's Gaelic name, and that by which the older inhabitants of the north still call it affectionately, is *Baile Dhuthaich*, or Duthus Town, after St. Duthus, the saint styled "Confessor of Ireland and Scotland," whose body was translated to Tain for burial in 1253. A rude, granite chapel "quhair he was borne," now roofless and dilapidated, bears his name, and was in ancient days a famous "girth," or sanctuary. Tain was frequently visited by royalty when the Stuarts ruled Scotland, but perhaps the most illustrious of those who came this way was Montrose. Captured in Assynt after his defeat at Carbisdale in 1650, he was brought prisoner to Tain and lodged in a house known as "The Ark." From Tain he went to Edinburgh, where he was sentenced to death on 20 May and hanged on the 21st.

STRANGE MOUNTAINS

THE mountains of Sutherland are unique in appearance as well as in origin. Their complex structure has attracted the attention of geologists from all parts of the world. If Canisp (at left of top picture) be the least interesting of them, Suilven (to right of Canisp), the Sugar Loaf, as it is often called, is certainly the most interesting. Lying five miles to the south-east of Lochinver, it completely dominates the surrounding country for many miles. When seen from east or west, it appears as a single, tapering cone, whereas in reality it consists of a long, narrow ridge divided into three main peaks. Loftiest of these is Caisteal Liath, or Grey Castle. Suilven ranks amongst the oddest, weirdest, and most inspiring natural phenomena in the land. Another remarkable mountain mass is Quinag (*left*). This mountain is situated in the Assynt region, and is known to rock-climbers and moun-

OF SUTHERLAND

taineers as the Water Stoup. Spidean Coinich, its southern peak, overlooks Loch Assynt, while Sail Gharbh, one of its western spurs, presents a magnificent face deeply lined by vertical gullies. On a spur of land jutting out from Loch Assynt are the ruins of Ardvreck Castle (*right*), where Montrose was imprisoned after his defeat at Carbisdale in 1650. His betrayal by Neil MacLeod, laird of Assynt, is to this day remembered with shame in the Scottish Highlands. Another imposing mountain mass is Ben Hope (*above*), situated at the south end of the loch of the same name. It is the most northerly summit in Britain exceeding 3,000 feet in height. It commands a fine view of the plains of Caithness, and of the Orkneys, lying beyond the Pentland Firth. Like most of the peaks in Sutherland it is far removed from inn or other habitation and is, therefore, beyond the reach of ordinary climbers.

117

CAPE WRATH, SUTHERLAND

CAPE WRATH, the extreme north-west point of the Scottish mainland, reminds one forcibly of the Butt of Lewis, and, like the Butt, it is surmounted by a lighthouse, built there in 1828. Both the north and west coasts of Sutherland, in its immediate locality, have a scenic grandeur not dissimilar to that of the more rugged parts of the Outer Hebrides. Bold and lofty cliffs, many of them honeycombed with caves, all of them the haunt of innumerable sea-birds— gulls, puffins, razorbills, shags, guillemots—rise precipitously from the tide's edge,

WICK HARBOUR, CAITHNESS

WICK is a seaport town consisting of three parts—Wick proper, which is the oldest part, Pulteneytown, on the south of Wick Bay, and Louisburgh, on the north side. Though Wick became a royal burgh in 1589, and county town of Caithness in 1641, it remained a place of little account until the rise of the fisheries toward the close of the eighteenth century. The port, which consists of two harbours, is now one of the most important fishing centres in Scotland. Among the interesting ruins in the locality are those of the old castle.

THE OLD MAN OF HOY, ORKNEY

THE only island of the Orkneys which attains an altitude of 1,000 feet above sea-level is Hoy. At its north-western end, where, through the centuries, the cliffs have been worn away to a height of about 400 feet, stands the Old Man of Hoy, one of the most famous sea-stacks in the world. Its height is 450 feet, and the distance at which it now stands from the rock curtain of which it once formed a part is some indication of its immense antiquity.

120

MAIN STREET, STROMNESS

SKIRTING a beautiful bay in the south-west of Pomona, the main island of the Orkneys, is the busy little town of Stromness. It is old, picturesque, and irregular, and so narrow are its pavementless thoroughfares that two vehicles cannot pass one another except at certain points, and only then with difficulty. Stromness has a population of roughly 1,600. Distilling, rope-making, boat-building, and herring fishing are its main industries.

ST. MAGNUS CATHEDRAL AND THE STANDING STONES

St. Magnus Cathedral (*left*) was founded in 1137, and dedicated to St. Magnus, who was executed at Egilsay in 1116. It dates from the time when the Orkneys were included in the See of Hamburg. It was not until about the middle of the twelfth century that they became a separate diocese in the ecclesiastical province of Nidaros, or Trondheim, in Norway. The Cathedral, which stands almost in the centre of the modern town of Kirkwall, ranks with Glasgow Cathedral as one of the two finest and most complete cathedral churches in Scotland. Among the best known of the innumerable ancient monuments preserved in the Orkneys are the Standing Stones of Stenness (*above*). Today there are no more than four of these massive, undressed monoliths, placed at regular intervals on the west arc of a circle believed to have comprised seven such stones.

A TYPICAL ORKNEY HOMESTEAD

ORKNEY, despite its remoteness and comparative shallowness of soil, is regarded by the Department of Agriculture for Scotland as one of the most productive and progressive agricultural regions in the country. It specializes in stock-raising and poultry, and has certain advantages over many rural counties in that its farms are small—on an average about thirty-four acres—and that the farmers and their families are usually able to work them without hired labour. Furthermore, no fewer than two-thirds of the Orcadian farms belong to their occupiers—a proportion much in excess of that to be found anywhere else. The climate is equable, and those who till the land are accessible to new ideas, and are seldom slow to avail themselves of the improved methods and implements of agriculture.

LERWICK HARBOUR, SHETLAND

LERWICK, county town of Shetland, stands on Bressay Sound, which, together with Lerwick Bay, forms one of the finest anchorages in Britain. The town dates only from the first half of the seventeenth century, though its appearance would lead one to assume a more ancient origin. By an Act of 1625 "anent the demolishing of the houssis of Lerwick," the Sheriff of Orkney and Shetland ordered that much of the town be laid waste because of the great wickedness of the inhabitants, and of the Dutch seamen resorting there in pursuit of the herring. Lerwick is one of the most important herring ports in the country. Every activity connected with the herring industry is carried on there. Its exports, in addition to enormous consignments of cured herrings, consist of knitted garments, cattle, sheep, and Shetland ponies.

SCALLOWAY AND SUMBURGH

HALF a dozen miles to the south-west of Lerwick lies the seaport village of Scalloway, once the capital of Shetland. The inhabitants are engaged in crofting and in fishing, and there is also a certain amount of boat-building and repairing. Here, at the head of a peninsula, stand the ruins of a castle (seen above), built by Patrick Stewart, the Tyrant of Orkney, to replace his earlier residence at Sumburgh, the foundations of which, resting on sand, began to subside. Sumburgh Head (*left*) is the most southerly point of Shetland. On the flat expanse to the north of the promontory is Shetland's airport. Round Sumburgh Head runs that powerful and menacing current known as the "Roost," the scene of the wreck from which Mordaunt Mertoun rescues Cleveland in Scott's novel, *The Pirate*.

THE ISLE OF MOUSA
AND ITS FAMOUS BROCH

THE island of Mousa (seen below) lies at no great distance from the east coast of Shetland's mainland, roughly midway between Lerwick and Sumburgh Head. Though today it is uninhabited, it once carried a population sufficient to warrant its having its own mill, and also a commodious kiln in which in olden days the islanders dried their corn. The island is now used solely for grazing, though evidences of tillage in earlier times are everywhere to be seen. It has a good, stone jetty at which small boats can disembark visitors who arrive from all parts of the world to examine its famous Broch, or prehistoric circular tower (seen at right), which has been preserved almost in a complete state, and is probably the most perfect antiquity of its kind in Europe. Its intramural galleries are still in excellent condition. It was taken over as a national monument in 1919.

INDEX TO PHOTOGRAPHS

ACKNOWLEDGEMENTS

The Editor is indebted to British Railways for permission to reproduce the picture appearing on page 7, and to Aerofilms, Limited, for the photographs on pages 71 and 86.